Looking at art

ABC

alphabet

■ national gallery of **australia**

Aa

apples

Ample apples
Picked from the tree
Are always so lovely
To eat and to see

Bb

boy

B is for boy
Dressed for Sunday play
Has he been bad
Or just a little sad?

Cc

cat

A cuddly cat
Stretching up
With curling tail
And eyes closed shut

Dd

dancers

Delicate dancers
Must follow the rules
When practising their turns
In dresses of tulle

Ee

easel

On the elegant easel
The picture rests
While the artists explain it
To the man on the left

Ff

flowers

Floaty flowers
With frowning faces
All bunched in a vase
They know their places

Gg

girl

Good little girl
Growing so tall
One day she'll be great
And go to a ball

Hh

hair

Halos of hair
Hanging so long
Holding the comb
She glides it along

li

inside

She sits in her room
In the middle of the day
I wonder if she'd rather
Go outside and play

Jj

jacket

In my jaunty jacket
I look jolly good
I'd tell you a joke
If only I could

Kk

kitchen

Chaos in the kitchen
Pears here and there
Right at the back
You can see a chair

Ll

lamp

Look at the little girl
As she looks at you
Under the lamp's light
She glows bright and new

Mm

mountain

Across the fields
Beyond the trees
Is a mighty mountain
Called Sainte-Victoire

Nn

night

Now it is night
And the stars shine bright
Reflecting on the water
They make beautiful light

Oo

onions

Old brown onions
Sitting on a plate
Might they be oval
Or round in shape?

Pp

piano

Playing the piano
This pretty girl
Poses for the painting
In her pink apron and single curl

Qq

quirky

Quirky and quaint
On her head a hat
Is she a queen?
I won't quarrel with that

Rr

resting

Rugged up in bed
And resting so warm
The covers pulled up
To sleep until dawn

Ss

ships

Against the sky
Full of colour
The tall ships sail sweetly
Into the harbour

Tt

top hat

His tip top hat
On his head
He's off to town
To buy some bread

Uu

umbrella

On a hot summer's day
She can stay cool
Under her umbrella
Lined with pale blue

Vv

vase

In a vertical vase
Or is it a jug?
The flowers look lovely
In violet and red

Ww

well

It's hard pulling water
Up from the well
Filling the jugs
To cart up the hill

X

X is a cross
X marks the spot
Words starting with X
There aren't a lot

Yy

yacht

Pale and soft
Floating and free
The yachts are so light
You can barely see

Zz

zigzag

Up and down
In and out
Side to side
That's what zig zags do

Paul Gauguin
Still-life with fan (Nature morte à l'éventail) c 1889
oil on canvas
50.0 x 61.0 cm
Musée d'Orsay, Paris, transferred in application of the Peace Treaty with Japan 1959, RF 1959-7
© RMN (Musée d'Orsay) / Hervé Lewandowski

Edgar Degas
Dancers climbing the stairs (Danseuses montant un escalier) 1886–90
oil on canvas
39.0 x 89.5 cm
Musée d'Orsay, Paris, bequest of Count Isaac de Camondo 1911, RF 1979
© RMN (Musée d'Orsay) / Hervé Lewandowski

Georges Seurat
The little peasant in blue (The jockey) (Le petit paysan en bleu (Le Jockey)) c 1882
oil on canvas
46.0 x 38.0 cm
Musée d'Orsay, Paris, gift of Robert Schmit 1982, RF 1982-54
© RMN (Musée d'Orsay) / Hervé Lewandowski

Maurice Denis
Homage to Cézanne (Hommage à Cézanne) 1900
oil on canvas
180.0 x 240.0 cm
Musée d'Orsay, Paris, gift of André Gide 1928, RF 1977-137
© RMN (Musée d'Orsay) / Hervé Lewandowski
© Maurice Denis. ADAGP/Licensed by Viscopy, 2009

Pierre Bonnard
The white cat (Le chat blanc) 1894
oil on card
51.0 x 33.0 cm
Musée d'Orsay, Paris, purchased 1982, RF 1982-74
© RMN (Musée d'Orsay) / Hervé Lewandowski
© Pierre Bonnard. ADAGP/Licensed by Viscopy, 2009

Vincent van Gogh
Imperial Crown fritillaries in a copper vase (Fritillaires couronne impériale dans un vase de cuivre) 1887
oil on canvas
73.0 x 60.5 cm
Musée d'Orsay, bequest of Count Isaac de Camondo 1911, RF 1989
© RMN (Musée d'Orsay) / Hervé Lewandowski

Edouard Vuillard
Public gardens: the question (Jardins public: l'interrogatoire) 1894
distemper on canvas
214.5 x 92.0 cm
Musée d'Orsay, Paris, bequest of Mrs Alexandre Radot 1978, RF 1978-47
© RMN (Musée d'Orsay) / Hervé Lewandowski
© Edouard Vuillard. ADAGP/Licensed by Viscopy, 2009

Vincent van Gogh
Eugène Boch or *The poet (Le poète)* 1888
oil on canvas
60.0 x 45.0 cm
Musée d'Orsay, Paris, bequest of Eugène Boch, through the Société des Amis du Louvre 1941, RF 1944-9
© RMN (Musée d'Orsay) / Hervé Lewandowski

Henri-Edmond Cross
Hair (La chevelure) c 1892
oil on canvas
61.0 x 46.0 cm
Musée d'Orsay, Paris, purchased 1969, RF 1977-128
© RMN (Musée d'Orsay) / Hervé Lewandowski

Paul Cézanne
Kitchen table (Still-life with basket) (La table de cuisine (Nature morte au panier)) 1888–90
oil on canvas
65.0 x 80.0 cm
Musée d'Orsay, Paris, bequest of Auguste Pellerin 1929, RF 2819
© RMN (Musée d'Orsay) / Hervé Lewandowski

Armand Seguin
Gabrielle Vien 1893
oil on canvas
88.0 x 115.0 cm
Musée d'Orsay, Paris, purchased 1929, RF 1977-313
© RMN (Musée d'Orsay) / Hervé Lewandowski

Félix Vallotton
Dinner, by lamplight (Le diner, effet de lampe) 1899
oil on card, laid on wood panel
57.0 x 89.5 cm
Musée d'Orsay, Paris, purchased 1947, RF 1977-349
© RMN (Musée d'Orsay) / Hervé Lewandowski

Paul Cézanne
Mount Sainte-Victoire (La Montagne Sainte-Victoire) c 1890
oil on canvas
65.0 x 92.0 cm
Musée d'Orsay, Paris, gift of the Pellerin family 1969, RF 1969-30
© RMN (Musée d'Orsay) / Hervé Lewandowski

Vincent van Gogh
Starry night (La nuit étoilée) 1888
oil on canvas
72.5 x 92.0 cm
Musée d'Orsay, Paris, gift of Mr and Mrs Robert Kahn-Sriber, in memory of Mr and Mrs Fernand Moch 1975, RF 1975-19
© RMN (Musée d'Orsay) / Hervé Lewandowski

Paul Cézanne
Still-life with onions (Nature morte aux oignons) 1896–98
oil on canvas
66.0 x 82.0 cm
Musée d'Orsay, Paris, bequest of Auguste Pellerin 1929, RF 2817
© RMN (Musée d'Orsay) / Hervé Lewandowski

Maurice Denis
*Princess Maleine's minuet (Marthe at the piano) (Le menuet de la princesse Maleine (Marthe au piano))*1891
oil on canvas
95.0 x 60.0 cm
Musée d'Orsay, Paris, accepted in lieu of tax 1999, RF 1999-3
© RMN (Musée d'Orsay) / Hervé Lewandowski
© Maurice Denis. ADAGP/Licensed by Viscopy, 2009

Edouard Vuillard
Profile of a woman in a green hat (Femme de profil au chapeau vert) c 1891
oil on card
21.0 x 16.0 cm
Musée d'Orsay, Paris, accepted in lieu of tax 1989, RF 1990-14
© RMN (Musée d'Orsay) / Hervé Lewandowski
© Edouard Vuillard. ADAGP/Licensed by Viscopy, 2009

Edouard Vuillard
In bed (Au lit) 1891
oil on canvas
73.0 x 92.5 cm
Musée d'Orsay, Paris, bequest of Edouard Vuillard carried out by Mr and Mrs Ker-Xavier Roussel 1941, RF 1977-374
© RMN (Musée d'Orsay) / Hervé Lewandowski
© Edouard Vuillard. ADAGP/Licensed by Viscopy, 2009

Paul Signac
Entry to the Port of Marseille (L'entrée du port de Marseille) 1911
oil on canvas
116.5 x 162.5 cm
Musée Cantini, Marseille, on long-term loan from the Musée d'Orsay, Paris, purchased 1912, RF 1977-324
Photograph: Jean Bernard

Paul Sérusier
*Still-life: the artist's studio (Nature morte: l'atelier de l'artiste)*1891
oil on canvas
60.0 x 73.0 cm
Musée d'Orsay, Paris, bequest of Henriette Boutaric 1984, RF 1984-11
© RMN (Musée d'Orsay) / Hervé Lewandowski

Pierre Bonnard
Portrait of Vuillard (Portrait de Vuillard) 1892
oil on wood panel
14.5 x 21.8 cm
Musée d'Orsay, Paris, purchased with the assistance of Philippe Meyer 1993, RF 1993-7
© RMN (Musée d'Orsay) / Hervé Lewandowski
© Pierre Bonnard. ADAGP/Licensed by Viscopy, 2009

Paul Signac
Women at the well or *Young women from Provence at the well, decoration for a panel in the shadows (Femmes au puits ou Jeunes provençales au puits, décoration pour un panneau dans la pénombre)* 1892
oil on canvas
195.0 x 131.0 cm
Musée d'Orsay, Paris, purchased 1979, RF 1979-5
© RMN (Musée d'Orsay) / Hervé Lewandowski

Henri Gervex
Madame Valtesse de La Bigne 1889
oil on canvas
200.0 x 122.0 cm
Musée d'Orsay, Paris, gift of Valtesse de la Bigne 1906, INV 20059
© RMN (Musée d'Orsay) / Hervé Lewandowski

Georges Seurat
France 1859–1891
Port-en-Bessin at high tide (Port-en-Bessin, avant-port, marée haute) 1888
oil on canvas
67.0 x 82.0 cm
Musée d'Orsay, Paris, purchased with funds from a Canadian anonymous gift 1952, RF 1952-1
© RMN (Musée d'Orsay) / Hervé Lewandowski

Vilhelm Hammershøi
Denmark 1864–1916
Rest (*Hvile*)1905
oil on canvas
49.5 x 46.5 cm
Musée d'Orsay, Paris, purchased with the
assistance of Philippe Meyer 1996, RF 1996-12
© RMN (Musée d'Orsay) / Michèle Bellot

Maurice Denis
France 1870–1943
Calvary (Climbing to Calvary) (*Le Calvaire
(La Montée au calvaire)*)1889
oil on canvas
41.0 x 32.5 cm
Musée d'Orsay, Paris, gift of Dominique Maurice-
Denis 1986, RF 1986-68
© RMN (Musée d'Orsay) / Hervé Lewandowski
© Maurice Denis. ADAGP/Licensed by Viscopy,
2009

nga.gov.au

Produced by NGA Publishing,
National Gallery of Australia

Writing and development: Julie Donaldson*
Design and production: Kirsty Morrison*
Rights and permissions: Nick Nicholson*
Pre-press and printing: Blue Star Print (Vic)
* National Gallery of Australia

National Library of Australia
Cataloguing-in-Publication
Title: ABC Alphabet
Edition: 1st ed
ISBN: 9780642334060 (hbk:1)
Series: Looking at art
Target audience: for pre-school age
Subjects: art appreciation–juvenile literature
Counting–juvenile literature
Other authors/contributors:
National Gallery of Australia
Dewey Number: 701.1

Published in conjunction with the exhibition
Masterpieces from Paris
Van Gogh, Gauguin, Cézanne and beyond
Post-Impressionism from the Musée d'Orsay
National Gallery of Australia, Canberra
4 December 2009 – 5 April 2010

 Musée
d'Orsay

Distributed in Australia by
Thames and Hudson
11 Central Boulevard Business Park
Port Melbourne, Victoria, 3207

Distributed in the United Kingdom by
Thames and Hudson 181A High Holborn
London WC1V 7QX, UK

Distributed in the United States of America by
University of Washington Press
1326 Fifth Avenue, Ste 555
Seattle, WA 98101-2604